Platinum |

Wise Publications
London/New York/Paris/Sydney/Copenhagen/Madrid/Tokyo

Exclusive Distributors:
Music Sales Limited
8/9 Frith Street, London W1D 3JB, England.
Music Sales Pty Limited
120 Rothschild Avenue, Rosebery, NSW 2018, Australia.

Order No. AM963809
ISBN 0-7119-8139-6
This book © Copyright 2000 by Wise Publications

Compiled and arranged by Stephen Duro
Music processed by Allegro Reproductions
Cover photographs courtesy of All Action and LFI

Printed and bound in Malta by Interprint Limited

Your Guarantee of Quality

As publishers, we strive to produce every book to the highest commercial standards.
This book has been carefully designed to minimise
awkward page turns and to make playing from it a real pleasure.
Particular care has been given to specifying acid-free, neutral-sized paper made from pulps
which have not been elemental chlorine bleached. This pulp is from farmed sustainable forests
and was produced with special regard for the environment.
Throughout, the printing and binding have been planned to ensure a sturdy, attractive publication
which should give years of enjoyment.
If your copy fails to meet our high standards, please inform us and we will gladly replace it.

Music Sales' complete catalogue describes thousands of titles and is available in full colour sections
by subject, direct from Music Sales Limited. Please state your areas of interest
and send a cheque/postal order for £1.50 for postage to:
Music Sales Limited, Newmarket Road, Bury St. Edmunds, Suffolk IP33 3YB.

www.musicsales.com

American Pie

Words & Music by Don McLean

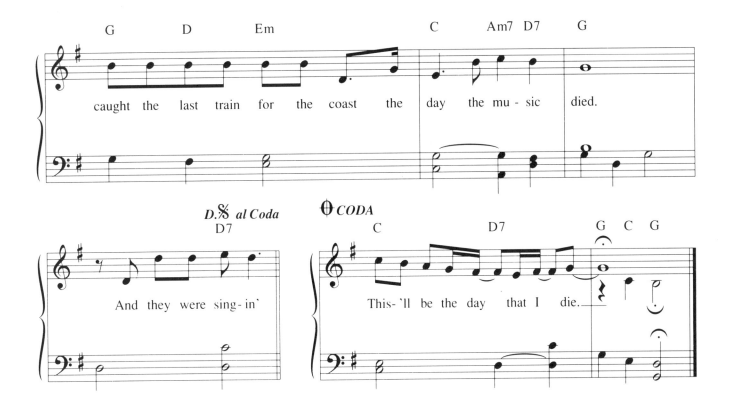

2. Now for ten years we've been on our own, and moss grows fat on a rollin' stone
   But that's not how it used to be when the jester sang for the king and queen
   In a coat he borrowed from James Dean and a voice that came from you and me
   Oh and while the King was looking down, the jester stole his thorny crown
   The courtroom was adjourned, no verdict was returned
   And while Lenin read a book on Marx the quartet practised in the park
   And we sang dirges in the dark
   The day the music died
   We were singin' . . . bye-bye . . . etc.

3. Helter-skelter in the summer swelter the birds flew off with a fallout shelter
   Eight miles high and fallin' fast, it landed foul on the grass
   The players tried for a forward pass, with the jester on the sidelines in a cast
   Now the half-time air was sweet perfume while the sergeants played a marching tune
   We all got up to dance but we never got the chance
   'Cause the players tried to take the field, the marching band refused to yield
   Do you recall what was revealed
   The day the music died
   We started singin' . . . bye-bye . . . etc.

4. And there we were all in one place, a generation lost in space
   With no time left to start again
   So come on, Jack be nimble, Jack be quick, Jack Flash sat on a candlestick
   'Cause fire is the devil's only friend
   And as I watched him on the stage my hands were clenched in fists of rage
   No angel born in hell could break that Satan's spell
   And as the flames climbed high into the night to light the sacrificial rite
   I saw Satan laughing with delight the day the music died.
   He was singin' . . . bye-bye . . . etc.

…Baby One More Time

Words & Music by Max Martin

Moderately

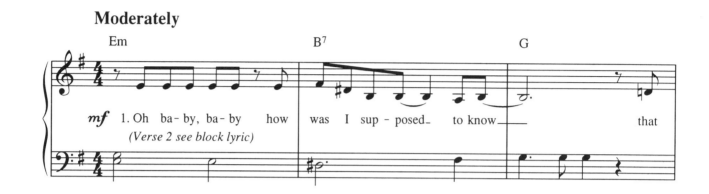

mf 1. Oh ba-by, ba-by how was I sup-posed to know that
(Verse 2 see block lyric)

some-thin' was-n't right here? Oh ba-by, ba-by I should-n't have let you go.

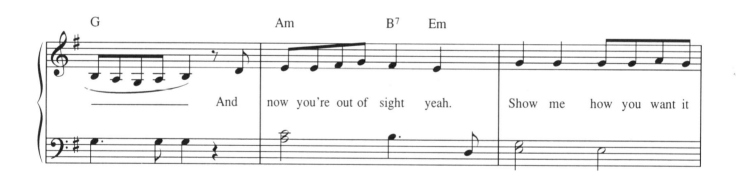

And now you're out of sight yeah. Show me how you want it

to be. Tell me ba-by 'cos I need to know now oh, be-cause

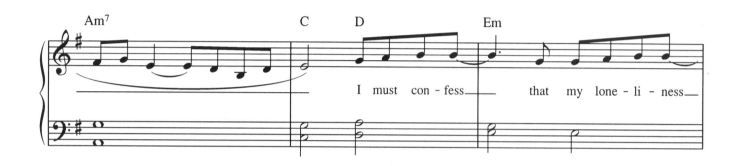

still be - lieve,_____ still be - lieve._____ When I'm not with you I lose

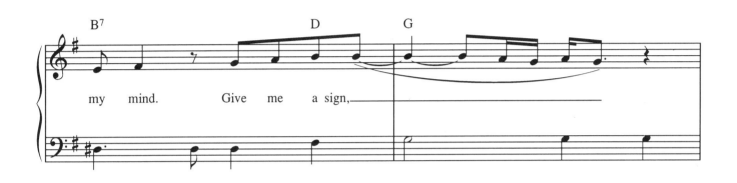

my mind. Give me a sign,_____

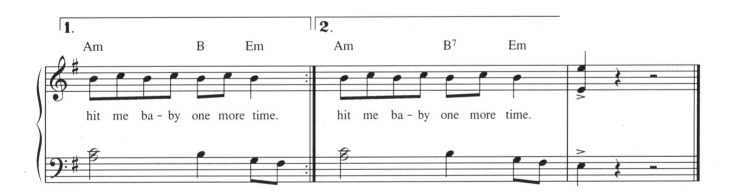

1. hit me ba - by one more time.

2. hit me ba - by one more time.

Verse 2:

Oh baby, baby
The reason I breathe is you
Boy you got me blinded.
Oh pretty baby
There's nothing that I wouldn't do
It's not the way I planned it.

Show me how you want it to be *etc*.

Common People

Words by Jarvis Cocker
Music by Pulp

Moderately bright

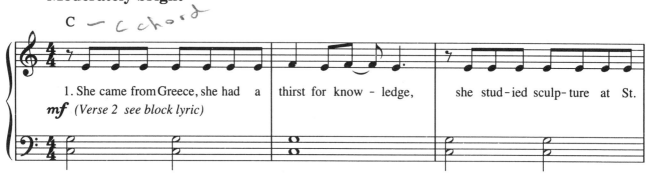

1. She came from Greece, she had a thirst for know-ledge, she stud-ied sculp-ture at St.

mf (Verse 2 see block lyric)

Mar-tin's col-lege that's where I caught her eye.

She told me that her dad was load-ed,

I said, in that case I'll have rum and Co-ca Co-la, she said, fine.

You'll nev-er live like com-mon peo-ple, you'll nev-er do what-

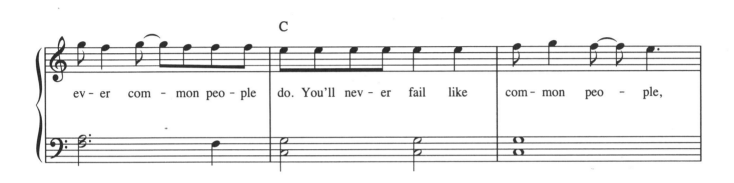

ev-er com-mon peo-ple do. You'll nev-er fail like com-mon peo-ple,

you'll nev-er watch your life slide out of view, and then dance and drink and

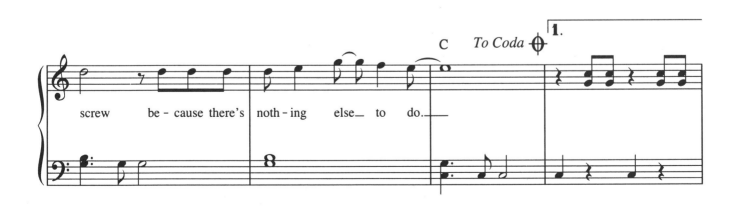

screw be-cause there's noth-ing else to do.

To Coda

1.

Want to live like com-mon peo - ple like you.

Verse 2:

I took her to a supermarket,
I don't know why
But I had to start it somewhere
So it started there.
I said pretend you've got no money
She just laughed and said oh you're so funny.
I said yeah?
Well I can't see anyone else smiling in here.
Are you sure you want to live like common people?
You want to see whatever common people see,
You want to sleep with common people,
You want to sleep with common people like me?
But she didn't understand;
She just smiled and held my hand.

Could It Be Magic

Words & Music by Barry Manilow & Adrienne Anderson

Moderately slow

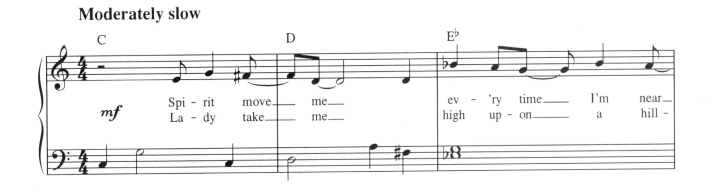

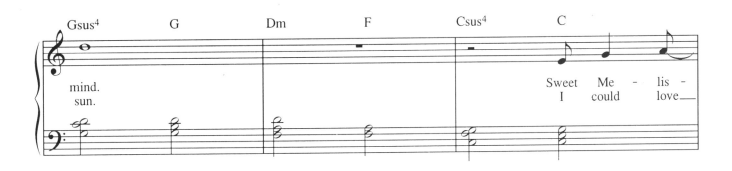

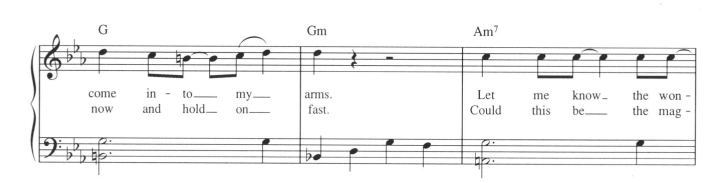

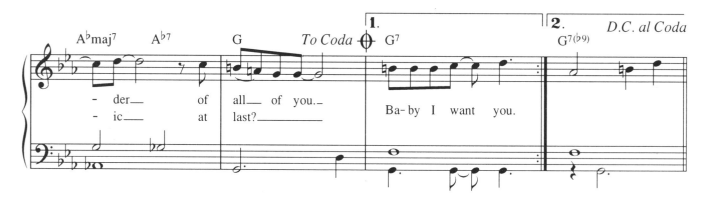

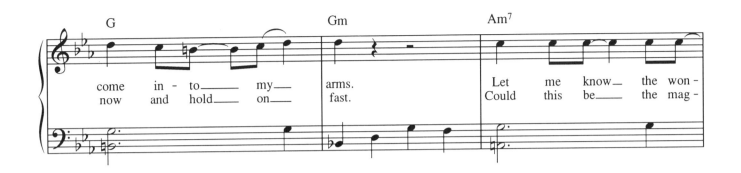

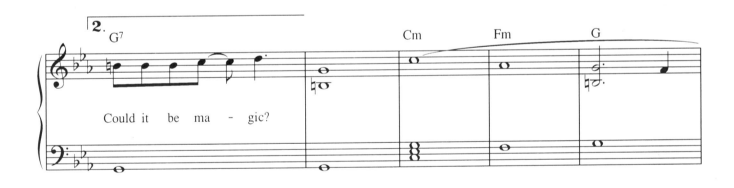

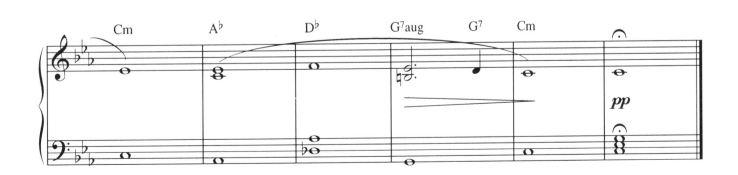

Every Breath You Take

Words & Music by Sting

ev-'ry game ___ you play, ___ ev-'ry night ___ you stay ___ I'll be watch-ing you.

(1.2.) Oh can't you see
(vocal each time)

that you be-long to me, my ___ poor heart ___

aches ___ with ev-'ry step ___ you take.

Ev-'ry move you ___ make, and ev-'ry vow you ___

(Everything I Do) I Do It For You

Words by Bryan Adams & Robert John 'Mutt' Lange
Music by Michael Kamen

Moderately

help___ it, there's no-thin' I want more. Yeah I would fight for you,___ I'd

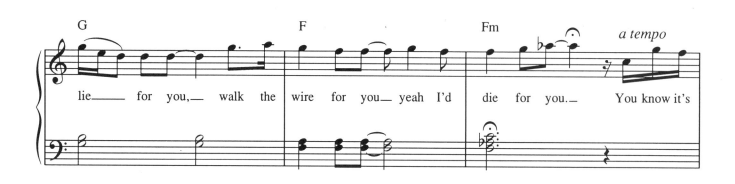

lie___ for you,___ walk the wire for you___ yeah I'd die for you.___ You know it's

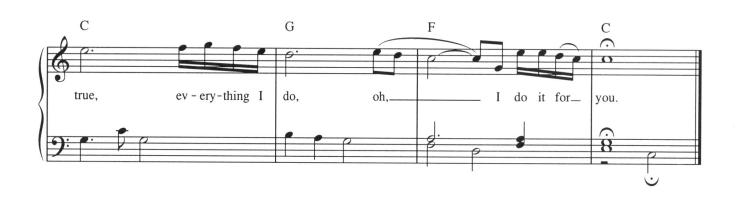

true, ev-ery-thing I do, oh,_____ I do it for___ you.

Verse 2:

Look into your heart
You will find there's nothin' there to hide
Take me as I am, take my life
I would give it all, I would sacrifice.

Don't tell me it's not worth fightin' for
I can't help it, there's nothin' I want more
You know it's true, everything I do
I do it for you.

Hero

Words & Music by Mariah Carey & Walter Afanasieff

Moderately

There's a he-ro___ if you look in-side your heart. You don't

long road___ when you face the world a-lone. No one

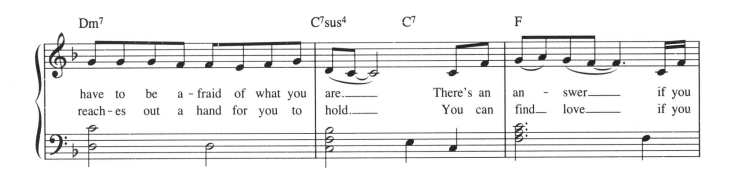

have to be a-fraid of what you are.___ There's an an-swer___ if you

reach-es out a hand for you to hold.___ You can find love___ if you

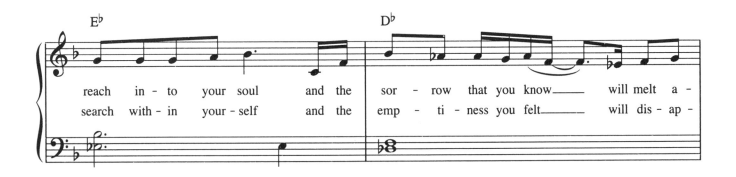

reach in-to your soul and the sor-row that you know___ will melt a-

search with-in your-self and the emp-ti-ness you felt___ will dis-ap-

way.
pear.

And then a he - ro comes a - long with the strength to car - ry

on and you cast your fears a - side and you know you can sur -

vive. So when you feel like hope is gone, look in - side you and be

strong. And you'll fin - ally see the truth, that a he - ro lies in

1. you._____

It's a

2. you._____

Lord_ knows_____

32

33

I Believe I Can Fly

Words & Music by R. Kelly

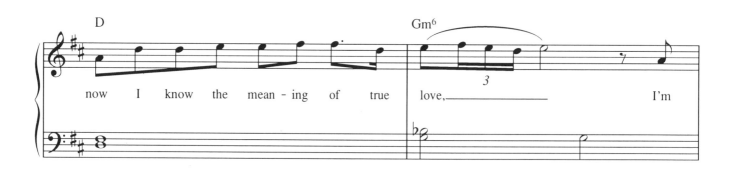

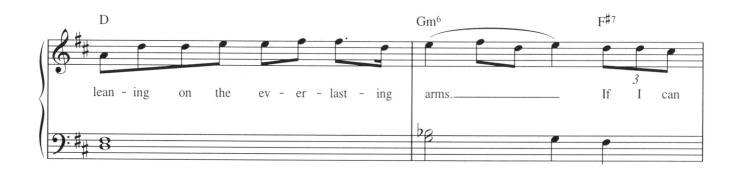

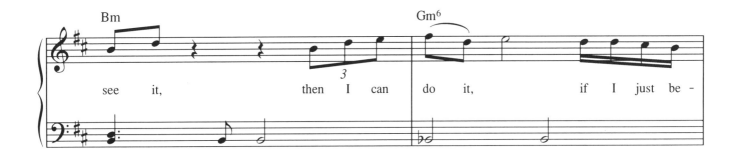

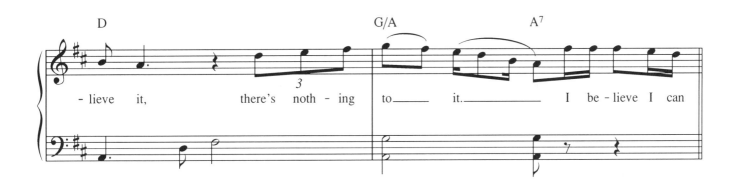

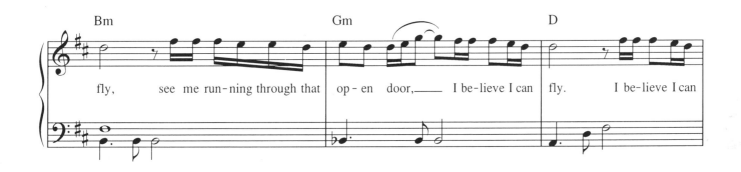

night and day,—— spread my wings and fly a - way,—— I be-lieve I can

soar, see me run - ning through that op - en door,———— I be-lieve I can

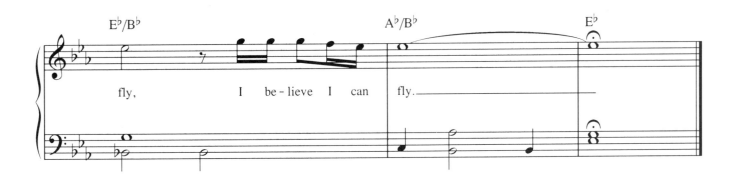

fly, I be - lieve I can fly.————

Verse 2:

See I was on the verge of breaking down,
Sometimes silence can seem so loud.
There are miracles in life I must achieve,
But first I know it stops inside of me.

Oh, if I can see it,
Then I can be it.
If I just believe it,
There's nothing to it.

I believe I can fly *etc.*

I Have A Dream

Words & Music by Benny Andersson & Björn Ulvaeus

Moderately

Love Is All Around

Words & Music by Reg Presley

Moderately

1. I feel it in my fin-gers, I feel it in my toes__
2. (see block lyric)

mf

The love that's all a-round me and so the feel-ing grows__

It's writ-ten on the wind, it's ev-'ry-where I go,__

So if you real-ly love me, come on and let it show__

Verse 2:

I see your face before me
As I lay on my bed;
I cannot get to thinking
Of all the things you said.
You gave your promise to me
And I gave mine to you;
I need someone beside me
In everything I do.

Perfect Moment

Words & Music by James Marr & Wendy Page

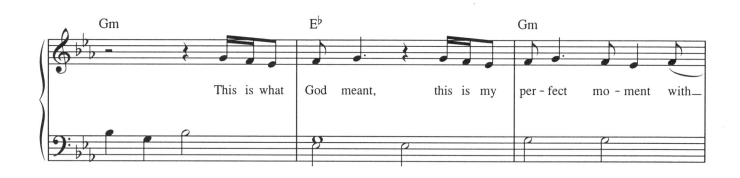

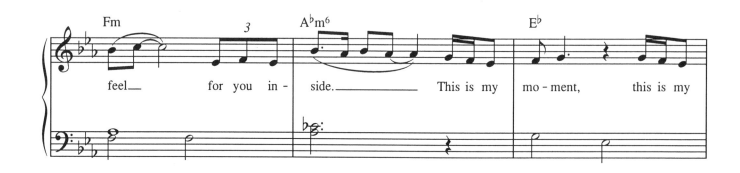

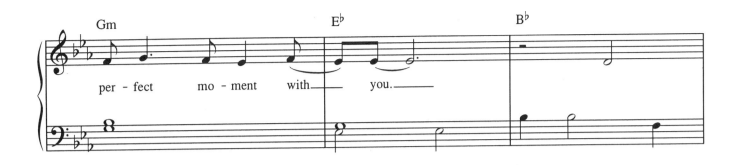

per - fect   mo - ment   with ___   you. ___

2. Tell me you love me   when you ___ leave.   You're more than a sha -dow,

that's what I ___ be - lieve.   You take me to pla -ces I ne -ver | thought I'd   see. ___

Min - ute by min -ute you're the | world   to me. ___ I wish I could | frame ___ the look in your

eyes, ___   the way that I | feel   for you in - | side. ___   This is my

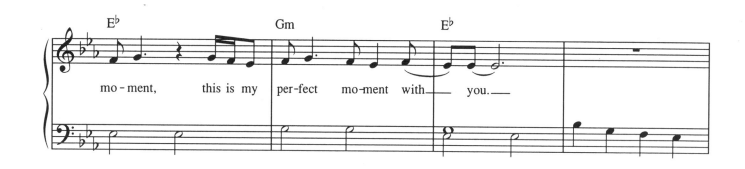

mo - ment, this is my per-fect mo-ment with____ you.____

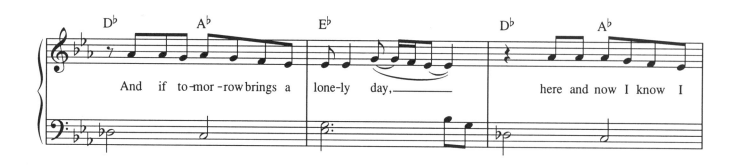

And if to-mor-row brings a lone-ly day,_____ here and now I know I

have - n't lived in vain. No more tears_ in the rain, and if love ne-ver comes a - gain I can

al -ways say I've been to pa - ra-dise skies in your eyes,_____

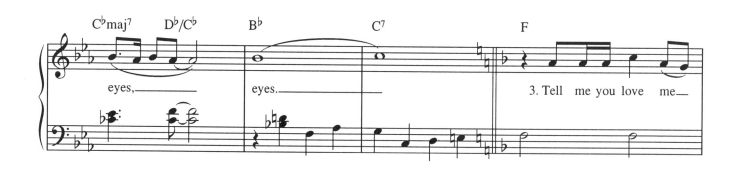

eyes,_____ eyes._____ 3. Tell me you love me____

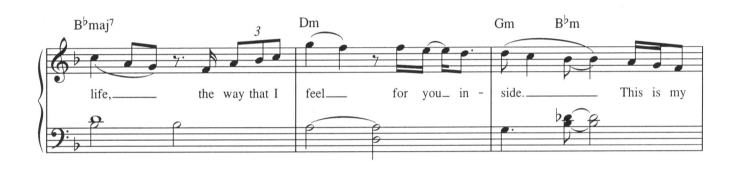

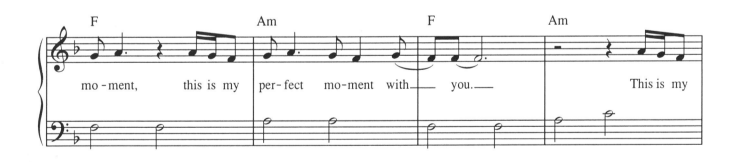

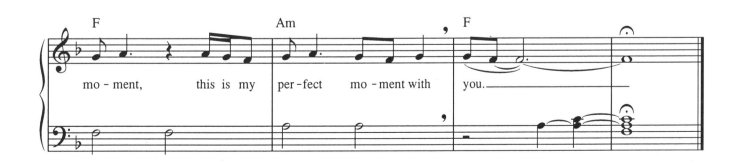

No Matter What

Words by Jim Steinman
Music by Andrew Lloyd Webber

Moderately

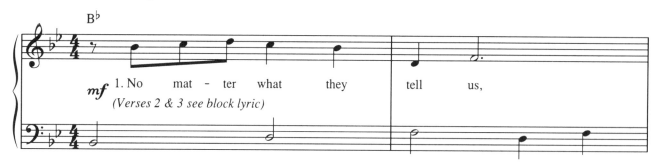

-tack, no mat - ter where they take us,

we'll find our own way back. I can't de - ny___ what

I be - lieve,___ I can't be___ what I'm not.___

1, 2.

I know our love's for - ev - er, I know no mat - ter

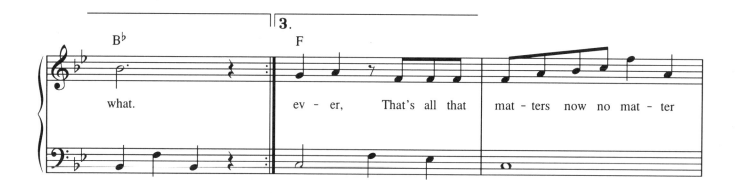

what.

ev - er, That's all that mat - ters now no mat - ter

what.

I know no mat - ter what.

Verse 2:

If only tears were laughter,
If only night was day,
If only prayers were answered
Then we would hear God say.
No matter what they tell us,
No matter what they do,
No matter what they teach you,
What you believe is true.
And I will keep you safe and strong
And sheltered from the storm.
No matter where it's barren
Our dream is being born.

Verse 3:
Instrumental:

No matter if the sun don't shine,
Or if the skies are blue.
No matter what the ending,
My life began with you.
I can't deny what I believe,
I can't be what I'm not.
I know this love's for ever,
That's all that matters now no matter what.

She's The One

Words & Music by Karl Wallinger

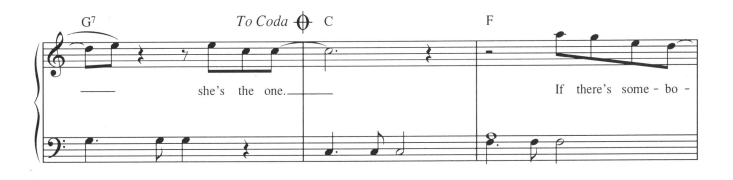

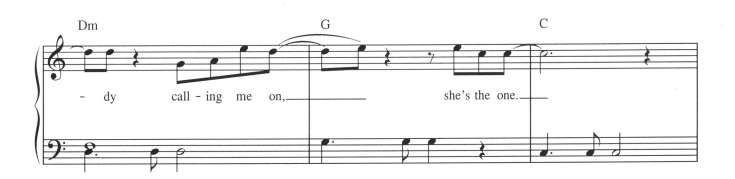

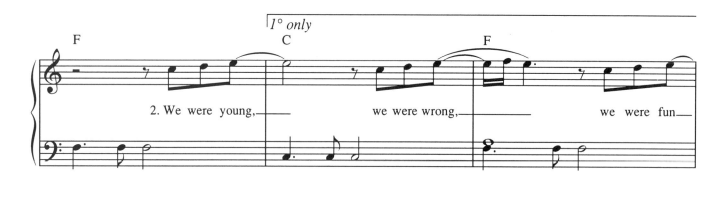

1° only

2. We were young,⎯ we were wrong,⎯ we were fun⎯

⎯ all a - long.⎯ If there's some - bo - dy call - ing me on,⎯

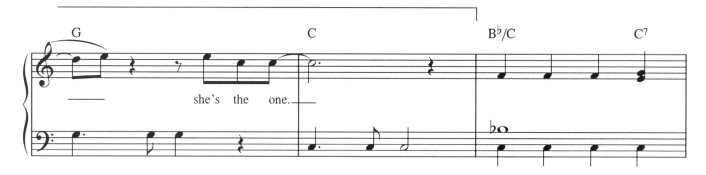

⎯ she's the one.⎯

When you get to where you wan - na go, and you know the things you wan - na know,⎯ you're

smil - ing.⎯ When you said what you wan - na say and you

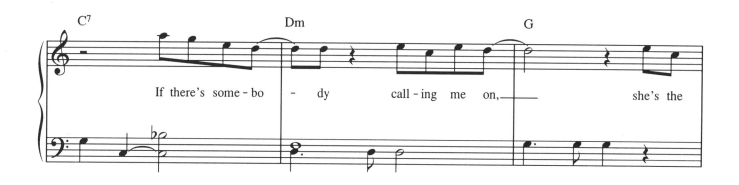

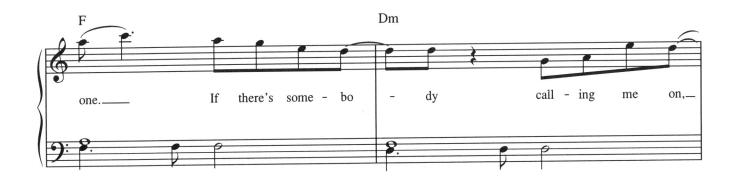

one.＿＿ If there's some - bo - dy call - ing me on,＿

she's the one.＿＿＿

She's the one.

Verse 3:

Though the sea will be strong
I know we'll carry on
'Cos if there's somebody calling me on, she's the one
If there's somebody calling me on, she's the one.

Verse 4:

I was her, she was me
We were one, we were free
And if there's somebody calling me on *etc.*

Stay Another Day

Words & Music by Tony Mortimer, Robert Kean & Dominic Hawken

love was gon - na be here___ to stay.

I've on - ly just be - gun to know you, all I can

say is won't you stay just one more day.___

2. stay.

Ba - by if you've got to go a - way don't think I can take the

Verse 2:

I touch your face while you are sleeping
And hold your hand
Don't understand what's going on
Good times we had return to haunt me
Though it's for you
All that I do seems to be wrong.

Tears In Heaven

Words & Music by Eric Clapton & Will Jennings

1. Would you know my name if I saw you in hea-ven?

Would you be the same if I saw you in hea-ven?

I must be strong

and car-ry on,_____ 'cause I know I don't be-

long_____ here in hea-ven.

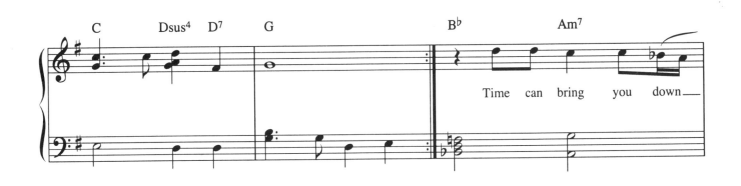

Time can bring you down_____

_____ time can bend your knees.

Time can break the heart ____ have you beg - ging, please, beg-ging, please.

CODA

- ven.

Verse 2:

Would you hold my hand
If I saw you in heaven?
Would you help me stand
If I saw you in heaven?
I'll find my way
Through night and day
'Cause I know I just can't stay
Here in heaven.

Verse 3: (D.S.)

Instrumental solo - 8 bars

Beyond the door
There's peace, I'm sure;
And I know there'll be no more
Tears in heaven.

Verse 4: (D.S.)

Would you know my name
If I saw you in heaven?
Would you be the same
If I saw you in heaven?
I must be strong
And carry on,
'Cause I know I don't belong
Here in heaven.

62

Think Twice

Words & Music by Andy Hill & Pete Sinfield

you— or us?— Ba - by,— don't say what you're a - bout to say,—

— look back be - fore you leave my life. Be sure be - fore you close that

Repeat to fade

door, be - fore you roll— those— dice. Don't

Verse 2:

Baby think twice, for the sake of our love,
For the memory,
For the fire and the faith
That was you and me.
Babe I know it ain't easy
When your soul cries out for higher ground,
'Cause when you're halfway up
You're always halfway down.

But baby this is serious,
Are you thinking 'bout you or us?

The Tide Is High

Words & Music by John Holt, Howard Barrett & Tyrone Evans

that.____ Oh, no._____ The tide is high but I'm

hold - ing on, I'm gon - na be your num - ber one.

To Coda ⊕

Num - ber one, Num - ber one.____

68

CODA

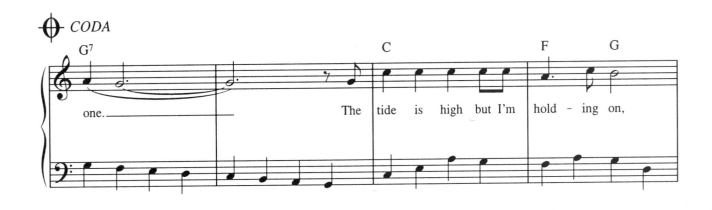

one._____ The tide is high but I'm hold - ing on,

I'm gon - na be your num - ber one. The tide is high but I'm

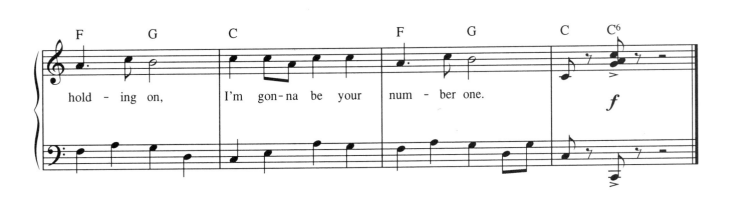

hold - ing on, I'm gon - na be your num - ber one.

The Way It Is

Words & Music by Bruce Hornsby

VERSE 2:

Said hey little boy you can't go
Where the others go
'Cause you don't look like they do
Said hey old man how can you stand
To think that way
Did you really think about it
Before you made the rules.
He said son

VERSE 2:

Well they passed the law in '64
To give those who ain't got a little more
But it only goes so far
Because the law don't change another's mind
When all it sees at the hiring time
Is the line on the colour bar oh no.

2 Become 1

Words & Music by Victoria Aadams, Melanie Brown, Emma Bunton, Melanie Chisholm, Geri Halliwell, Matt Rowe & Richard Stannard

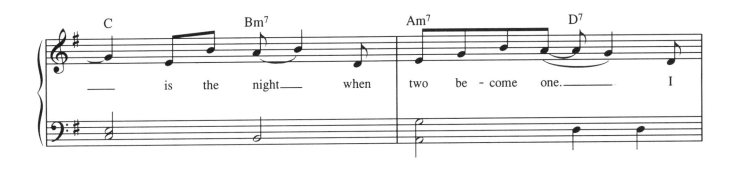

is the night___ when two be - come one._____ I

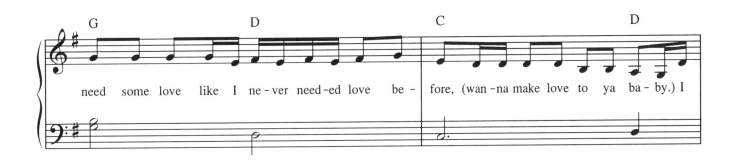

need some love like I ne - ver need -ed love be - | fore, (wan -na make love to ya ba - by.) I

had a lit - tle love now I'm back for | more, (wan -na make love to ya ba - by.)

set your spi - rit free, it's the | on - ly way to be.___

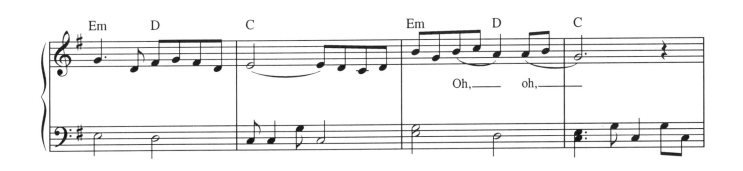

Oh,___ oh,___

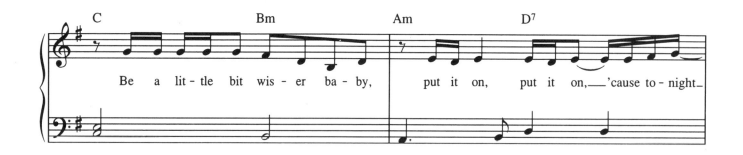

Be a lit-tle bit wis-er ba-by, put it on, put it on,—'cause to-night—

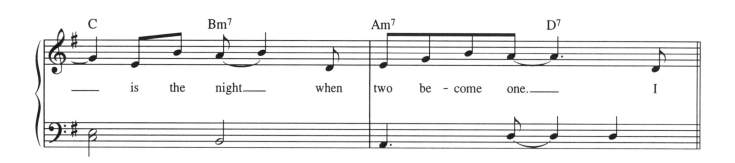

— is the night—— when two be-come one.—— I

need some love like I ne-ver need-ed love be-fore, (wan-na make love to ya ba-by.) I

Repeat to fade

had a lit-tle love now I'm back for more, (wan-na make love to ya ba-by.) I

Verse 2:

Silly games that you were playing, empty words we both were saying,
Let's work it out boy, let's work it out boy.
Any deal that we endeavour, boys and girls feel good together,
Take it or leave it, take it or leave it.
Are you as good as I remember baby, get it on, get it on,
'Cause tonight is the night when two become one.

I need some love like I never needed love before, (wanna make love to ya baby.)
I had a little love, now I'm back for more, (wanna make love to ya baby.)
Set your spirit free, it's the only way to be.

When You Say Nothing At All

Words & Music by Paul Overstreet & Don Schlitz

Moderately

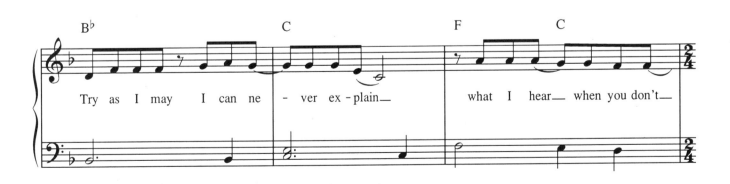

— me wher - ev - er I fall.

You__ say it best when you say no - thing at all.__

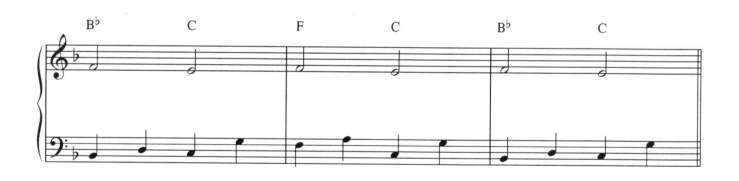

(You say it best__ when you say__ no - thing at all.__)

(You say it best___ when you say___ no - thing at all.___) That

smile on your face,___ there's truth in your eyes.___ The

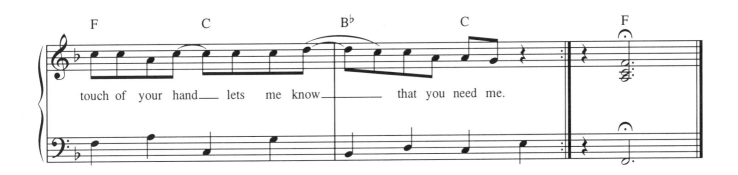

touch of your hand___ lets me know___ that you need me.

Verse 2:

All day long I can hear people talking out loud
But when you hold me you drown out the crowd
Try as they may they can never defy
What's been said between your heart and mine.

The smile on your face *etc.*

What Can I Do

Words & Music by Andrea Corr, Caroline Corr, Sharon Corr & Jim Corr

Moderately

I have-n't slept at all in days,
(Verse 2 see block lyric)

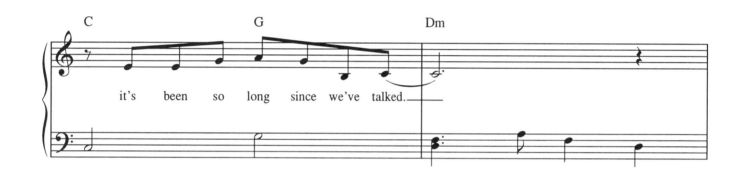

it's been so long since we've talked.

And I have been here ma - ny times

I just don't know what I'm do - ing wrong.

What can I do to make you love me?

What can I do to make you care?

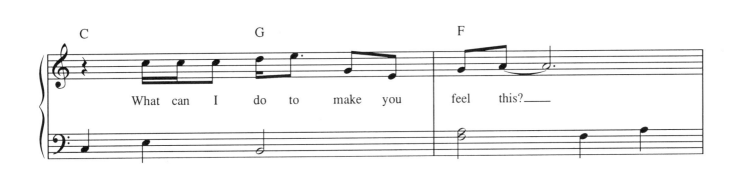

What can I do to make you feel this?

To Coda ⊕

What can I do to get you there?

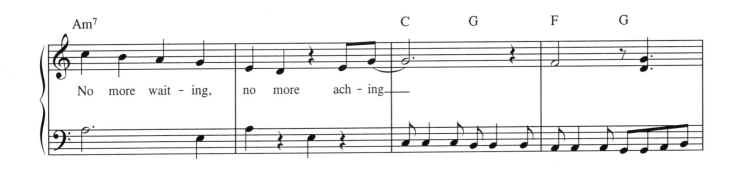

No more wait - ing, no more ach - ing

Love me,—— love me,—— love—— love me,——

love me,—— love—— love me,—— love me,—— love——

love me,—— love me,—— love—— love me.

Verse 2:

There's only so much I can take
And I just got to let it go
And who knows I might feel better
If I don't try and I don't hope.

What can I do...

You Are Not Alone

Words & Music by Robert Kelly

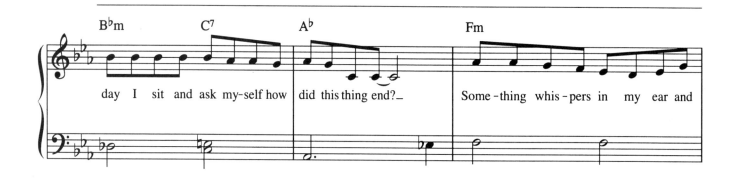

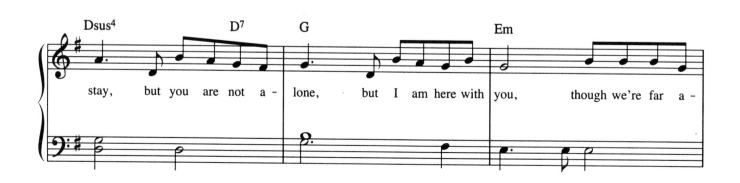

part, you're al - ways in my heart, you are not a - lone.

Repeat ad lib. to fade

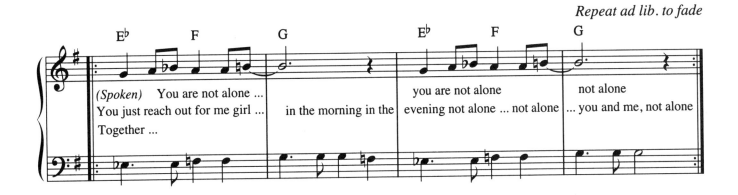

(Spoken) You are not alone ...
You just reach out for me girl ...
Together ...

you are not alone

not alone

in the morning in the | evening not alone ... not alone | ... you and me, not alone

Verse 2:

You are not alone
I am here with you
Though you're far away
I am here to stay.
You are not alone
I am here with you
Though we're far apart
You're aways in my heart.
But you are not alone.

Verse 3:

Just the other night
I thought I heard you cry
Asking me to go
And hold you in my arms.
I can hear your breaths
Your burdens I will bear
But first I need you here
Then forever can begin.

Verse 4:

You are not alone
I am here with you
Though you're far away
I am here to stay.
But you are not alone
But I am here with you
Though we're far apart
You're always in my heart.
But you are not alone.

You Gotta Be

Words & Melody by Des'ree
Music by Ashley Ingram

Moderately

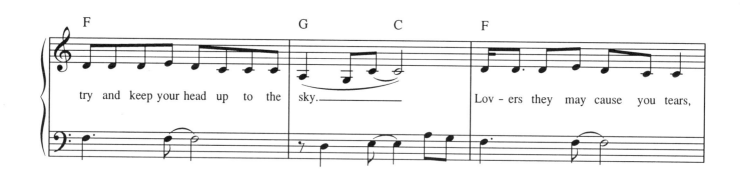

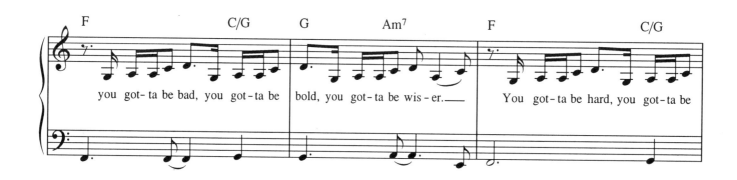

you got-ta be bad, you got-ta be bold, you got-ta be wis-er.

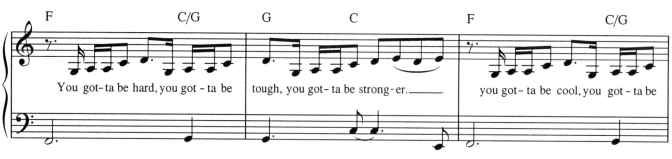

You got-ta be hard, you got-ta be tough, you got-ta be strong-er. you got-ta be cool, you got-ta be

calm, you got-ta stay to-geth-er. All I know, all I know love will save the day.

Time asks no ques-tions, it goes on with-out you, leav-ing you be-hind if you can't

stand the pace, The world keeps on spin-ning, can't stop it if you tried to. The

Verse 3:

Remember listen as your day unfolds
Challenge what the future holds
Try to keep your head up to the sky
Lovers they may cause you tears
Go ahead release your fears.
My, oh my, hey hey.

Why Does It Always Rain On Me?

Words & Music by Fran Healy

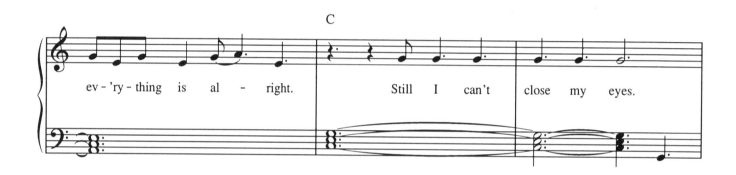

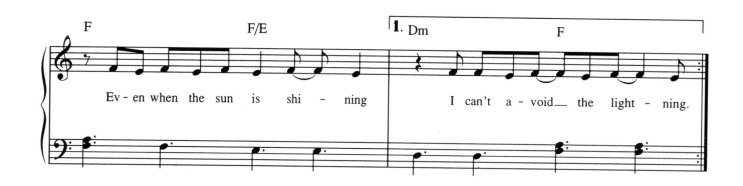

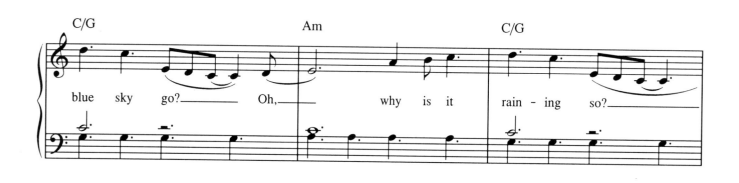

🔶 *CODA*

It's so _____ cold. _____

Why does it al - ways rain on __ me? Is it be - cause I

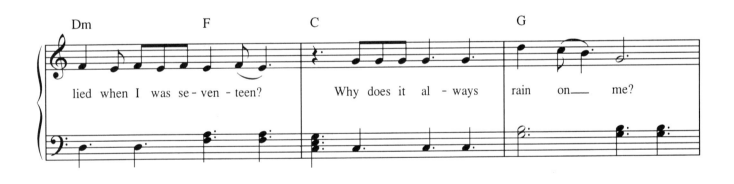

lied when I was se - ven - teen? Why does it al - ways rain on __ me?

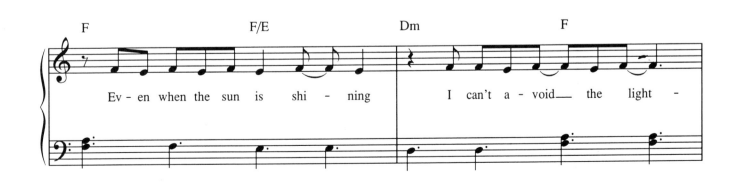

Ev - en when the sun is shi - ning I can't a - void __ the light -

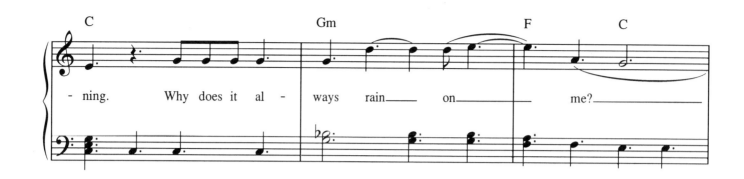

-ning.   Why does it al - ways rain___ on___   me?___

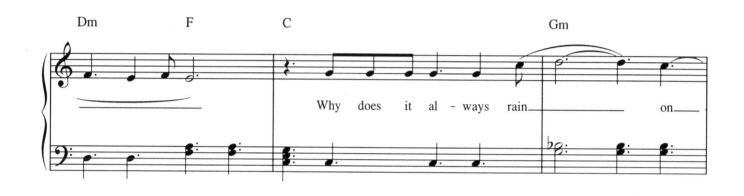

Why does it al - ways rain___ on___

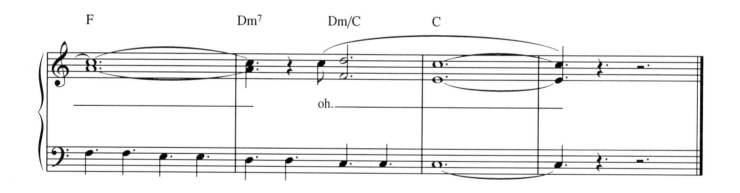

oh.___

Verse 2:

I can't stand myself
I'm being held up by invisible men
Still life on a shelf when
I got my mind on something else
Sunny days, where have you gone?
I get the strangest feeling you belong.

Why does it always rain on me *etc.*

12/03 (49670)